Thriving Corporate Consciousness

Diane Hewat

BookLeaf Publishing

India | USA | UK

Thriving Corporate Consciousness © 2021

Diane Hewat

All rights reserved.

No part of this publication may be reproduced, stored in a retrieval system, or transmitted, in any form or by any means, electronic, mechanical, photocopying, recording or otherwise, without the prior written permission of the presenters.

Diane Hewat asserts the moral right to be identified as the author of this work.

Presentation by *BookLeaf Publishing*

Web: www.bookleafpub.com

E-mail: info@bookleafpub.com

ISBN: 9789357447454

First edition 2021

To my clients - together we are contributing to thrivability. We are raising corporate consciousness, one conversation at a time.

ACKNOWLEDGEMENT

To my daughter, who encouraged me to write this book.

To my clients, acknowledging their creativity, care and courage.

PREFACE

My soon-to-be daughter-in-law sparked the first poem in this book. As a young professional, she became incensed with the way people in her organisation were being treated.

The rest of the poems are a blend of my personal experiences and those of the clients I have had the good fortune to work with over the last 2 decades.

The poems are a mix of low and high levels of consciousness. The high levels of consciousness enable both people and their organisations to thrive.

Discarded

For 23 years they had been
The heart and soul of their teams.
First to arrive
Last to leave
Dependable, reliable, responsible.

One sunny, spring afternoon
All were called to a company-wide Zoom.
New structures, new roles, new jobs.
Their names? Absent from all logs.

Disbelief, anger, hurt and sadness
Emptiness.
Then, the memories.
Sacrifices, commitments.
Defending others' decisions to disgruntled staff.
Broken marriages.
The missed…
School concerts, birthday parties,
Drop-offs, pick-ups, sports games,
Parent-teacher meetings, school plays.

The years of unpaid overtime
Believing in the company line

Not a word

Not a hint
Not a whisper of thanks for
The results delivered,
The secrets kept,
The skeletons hidden.

The sadness, deep and slow, unbidden
Rises through the betrayal pain.
With a glimmer, strange pinpoint
Of relief wrapped within the shame.

Relating

Soft are the winds that carry me
From client to office and industry
Gentle the bonds that tie and bind
Relationships through space and time

Joy is the sense that spurs me on
From chaos to order till the job's done
Faith is the joy that brings us fun
As together we achieve what we could not as
one.

Once Upon A Time

Once upon a time
There was a thought
A dream
A vision
That the world could be a better place.

People gathered together
Hope shining across
Their collective face.

With passion, with purpose
Their bonds became strong
Together they toiled
Learning to get along.

Time slowly eroded
The vision shared
Air leaking from a tyre
Because nobody cared.

Greeting

8

Good morning!
They said
With a lift of their head,
A gentle smile
Stays for a while
The light in their eyes
A joyful prize
Starting our new day.

If Only

If only the organisation knew
What the people in the organisation know.

The skills they are hired for
Are but grains of sand
In the true wealth they bring.

The true wealth of
Compassion,
Kindness,
Creativity and
Courage.

The potential where
Care for each other
The warming of hearts
The human connection
Catapults performance
Empowering the
Human Race.

How do I find this?

12

Beyond the skills
Beyond the roles
Beyond the toll
Of quarterly goals

There lies a field
Of wealth untold
Available through
Caring for the whole

How do I find this?

Assumptions

I woke this morning with feelings of dread.
With thoughts of my day pounding through my
head.
The blaming, the complaining
The finger-pointing, the shaming.

The assumptions they're making
Have my confidence quaking
The conclusions they're drawing
Have me with-drawing. Shaking.

I don't want to do it.
I don't want to go.
To a place I don't fit.
Where they don't want to know
The reasons behind
The things that I do.
Where all minds are closed
To anything new.

If...

If I were to sing a song of joy,
What would it be?

If I were to paint the vibrance of love,
What would I see?

If I were to live my soul's best life
What would I hear?

If I were to belong to one great team
What would be clear?

Helpless

I've just been in a meeting
With inadequate seating
Where a new trainee
Was shamed – for all to see.

I feel so helpless.
An emotional mess.
It's so unfair,
What they did in there.

How could anyone know
The unwritten rules?
How is it ok for them
To be so cruel?

Little Things

20

It's the little things
That make life worthwhile.
The nod of a head
A kind glance, a smile.

Appreciation of
A job well done.
Acknowledgment of
Journeys begun.

Assumptions

I woke this morning
With feelings of dread
With thoughts of my day
Streaming through my head
The blaming, the complaining
The finger point shaming.

The assumptions they're making
Have my confidence shaking
The conclusions they're drawing
Have my inner system quaking.

I don't want to do it
I don't want to go
To a place I don't fit
Where they don't want to know
The reasons behind
The things that I do
Where naming blaming and complaining
Belittle and shame me.

Imagining

I imagine, as I work
Feeling safe
Feeling seen
Feeling heard
Feeling valued
Feeling my contribution matters
Feeling my contribution makes a difference
Feeling my opinion matters
Feeling motivated
Feeling I make a difference

Feeling I belong

I imagine as I leave work for the day
Feeling more energised than when I arrived.

Feeling Unsafe

I'm sitting at my window
Looking out at the fence
Playing with the words
Fence and defence.

Knowing both are about protection
In the outer world and inner
And somehow, the latter
Isn't working.

The scene plays over
In my head
She said… he said…
And finding – I felt…

I felt attacked
I felt afraid
I felt trapped
In this job
I have to do
To pay the bills.

Feeling Seen

"Well done!" my leader said.
"Thank you!" I replied, curious, waiting.
My leader said,
"In that meeting,
In the heated discussion,
You waited,
As things escalated
Tempers flared.
Arguments turned into shouts.
You watched. You listened.
You went to the board.
You wrote the core of the opposing views.
Then added a third as they continued.
Respectfully
You drew their attention.
Within seconds
Animosity evaporated.
They started thinking and exploring
New options.

Your quiet approach
Your actions
Not only deescalated
But quickly moved them from
Being adversarial into
Being cooperative.

Well done!"

I feel seen.

No Way Out

It's like this big black cloud
Is following me
From task to task
Conversation to conversation
Document to document.

I have to get things done.
I have to meet deadlines.
I have to meet targets.
Where's the time and space for me?

Feeling Heard

"Well done!" my leader said.
"Thank you!" I replied, curious, waiting.

"In the meeting, you summarised
Points of view, added your own perspective
And identified 3 recommendations.
Two were accepted, one was adapted.
Well done!"

I feel heard.

Chastised

I've just been told off
For something I didn't do.

I had to sit there and listen
To conclusions drawn.

Why do people do this?
Why, oh why
Do they see half a story
And in their mind
Construct so much nastiness
Around what they find?

I see work values
Up on the wall.
Are they really intended
To have me playing this small?

Feeling Valued

"Come in!" smiled
My leader to me,
Moving to my side of the desk.

Sitting in a visitor's chair
"How'd you feel,
You have progressed?"
I paused a moment as
My brain processed.

"Really well, most of the time,
I'm able to deliver my best.

Eyes meeting mine warmed with
Deep respect.

"Our clients tell me
Your work's top notch."

Through this feedback, short, direct
I felt valued.

Drudgery

So much to do
So little time
Going to work
Every day is a grind

Alarm goes off
Feelings of dread
Force myself to get up
Don't make my bed

Drag my feet through the day
Wishing the drudgery
Would just
Go away.

My Contribution Matters

"Well done!" my leader said.
"Thank you!" I replied, curious, waiting.

"In the meeting with our client,
I noticed they were really frustrated.
You asked them a question,
Not judging,
Not threatening,
You built on their answers
By asking more questions.
Clarifying. For them, for us.

When I would have stopped,
You continued.
We left the meeting
With clear actions
Not only what to do
But why we were doing them.

WE moved from them and us.
To we.

Together, we created
A course of action
That I would never have thought of.
That is far simpler, quicker and cost effective

Than what I had come up with myself.

Well done!"

I felt my contribution mattered.

Improving Lives

44

I imagine a world where I'm part of a team
Where the work I do is valued and seen
Where the people I work with are where I
belong
All in one corporate choir, we sing the same
song

Where each contribution is shared and revered
Healing our planet where all damage is cleared
Imagine our outputs improving the lives
Of all humanity's man, woman and child.